AF505683

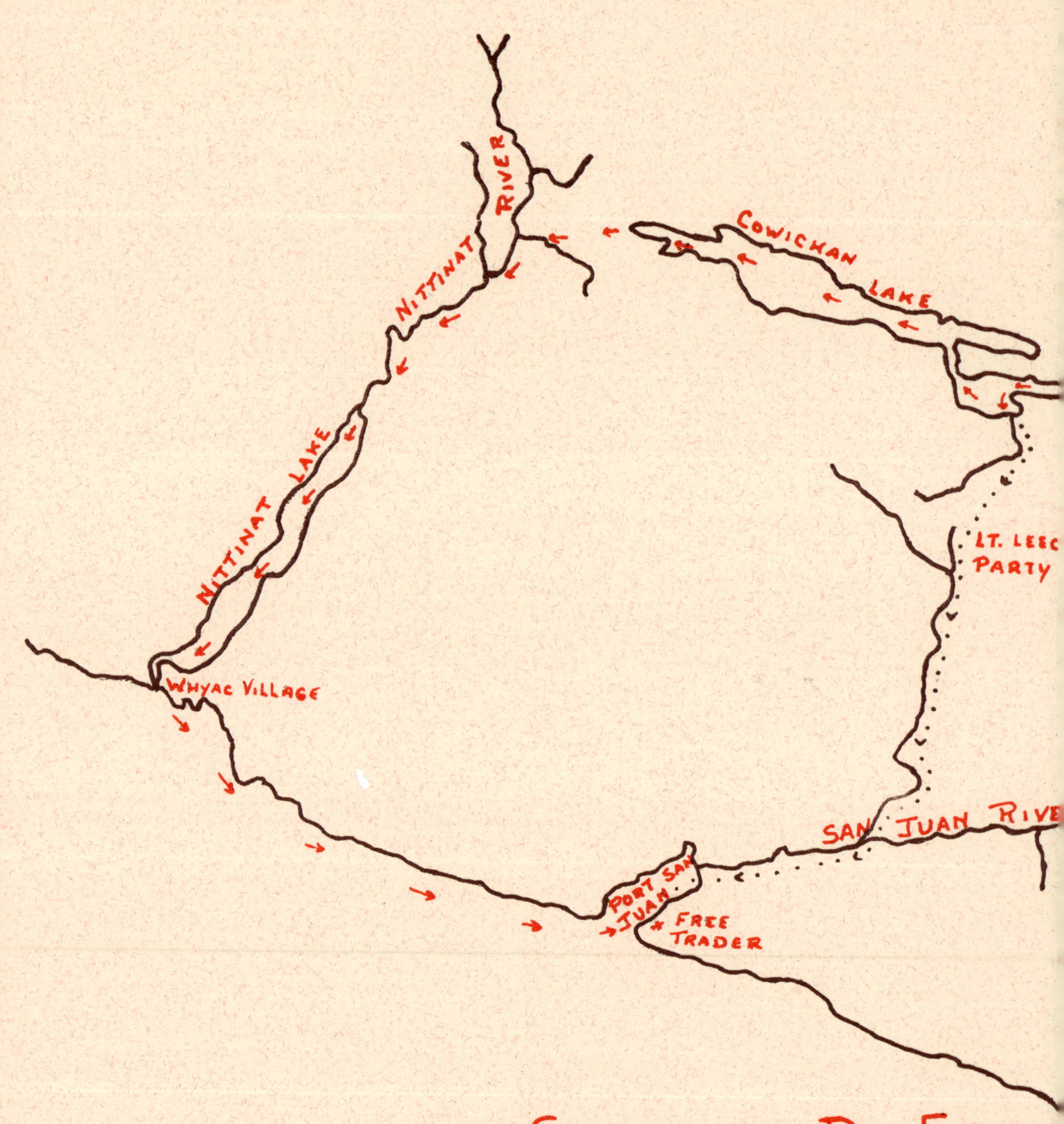

NITTINAT RIVER
COWICHAN LAKE
NITTINAT LAKE
LT. LEECH PARTY
WHYAC VILLAGE
SAN JUAN RIVER
PORT SAN JUAN
FREE TRADER
STRAITS OF DE FUCA

SALT
SPRING
ISL.
Cowichan River
VANCOUVER ISLAND
Victoria

FIRST JOURNEY OF EXPLORATION
ACROSS VANCOUVER ISLAND

FIRST JOURNEY OF EXPLORATION ACROSS VANCOUVER ISLAND

BY

ROBERT BROWN F.R.G.S. Etc.,

Commander of the Expedition

YE GALLEON PRESS
FAIRFIELD, WASHINGTON 99012

INTRODUCTION

It was in the spring of 1863 that Robert Brown, then 22 years old and fresh from the University of Edinburgh, arrived in Victoria. He had been sent out by the Botanical Association of Edinburgh to collect seeds and plants in the Colony of Vancouver Island. The fall and summer of 1863 were spent collecting along the west coast as far north as Nootka Sound and into the area of Great Central Lake near Alberni.

In the spring of 1864 Arthur Kennedy, Governor of Vancouver Island, encouraged the formation of an ''exploring expedition'' that would travel the length and breadth of the island revealing its secrets. Brown actively pursued the appointment of Commander, and on the 1st. of June 1864 the organizing committee, comprising some of Victoria's leading citizens, gave him the position.

The committee then picked the members of the party, each having a particular expertise, to ensure the success of the expedition. Lieutenant Peter Leech, who had come to the Colony with the Royal Engineers, was appointed second-in-command. Frederick Whymper was to fill the bill as an artist, sketching some thirty drawings while with the expedition. Henry Thomas Lewis was a graduate of Cambridge University and claimed to have farming experience. Alexander Barnston, a Canadian, graduated from McGill University and was described as an all around outdoors-man. John Meade, who also came out with the Royal Engineers, was amoung the first chosen. John Foley, an American, had practical experience in hard rock and placer mining. Ranald MacDonald, born on the north-west coast to a Chief Factor of the Hudson's Bay Company and a daughter of Comcomly, Chief of the Chinook, for his understanding of the Indians. John Buttle a botanist with the British North American Boundary Commission.

While the trip up the Cowichian River and down to the Nitinat Lake was only a part of the exploration of Vancouver Island carried out by Brown during the summer and fall of 1864, it is the part told first in *Illustrated Travells* and retold here for your enjoyment.

INNES L. COOPER
January 30, 1987
Victoria, B.C.

FIRST JOURNEY OF EXPLORATION ACROSS VANCOUVER ISLAND was originally written by Robert Brown for the magazine:

ILLUSTRATED TRAVELLS;
a record of Discovery
Geography and Adventure.

Published by Cassell, Petter and Galpin
London, England 1869

THANKS IS GIVEN TO:

Mr. John Hayman for his help in the preparation of the introduction, and

the Provincial Archives of British Columbia for providing access to the Brown material, and for the 35 mm colour slide pdp. 1704 of Camp Lake Cowichian.

N EXPLORING EXPEDITION IN THE FAR West, amoung (sic) the wooded mountains, great lakes, and rapid rivers of the distant shores of the North Pacific, is a very different matter from similar enterprises starting well-founded, well-considered, and properly equipped from England. In the little frontier town where we start from, there are no philosophical instrument-makers to advise us with the tools for our work, no Geographical Society to advise us, and we miss the kindly God-speed of Sir Roderick. Apparatus has to be extemporised and men found at a short notice. There is certainly no want of applicants, but though we only want 10, upwards of 100 besiege the doors of our committee-room, in the city of Victoria, Vancouver Island. Every member of that local board seems anxious to select his own friends, or those whom he may suppose to be friendly to his interests; but, as the leader has to work this heterogeneous team, he also has to cut the Gordian knot by selecting them himself, in the short week which elapses from the day of his selection until the day of starting.

A queer-looking lot they are universally pronounced (in stage whispers) to be, as they are mustered that bright June morning to hear the Governor's farewell advice. Most of them have been up all night, celebrating their departure after the approved north-western fashion, and late hours and frequent toasts have not improved the personal appearance of the first Vancouver Exploring Expedition. Dark, hawk-eyed half breeds, quick of limb and stubborn of temper, stand side by side with miners from Cornwall and lumber-men from Canada, who jostle, in their turn, more than one Oxford graduate who, in many a long experience of wild north-western life, have come out double-first in wood-craft, and, save for a more intelligent air, would be hard to distinguish from their unlettered companions. We have a clergyman who, in his younger days, was given to Ritualism, but for many a year has hunted bear and elk, beaver and the black-tailed deer, as a profession; and an artist, very good in his way, who has for some time past been more familiar with the gold-miner's pick than the painter's palette. They are of all ages—from one and twenty to one and forty—and no two are exactly of one nationality; religion we don't dispute much about. To keep law and order over this strange mob, and out of chaos to bring light geographical, I was appointed sole commander. Our duty is to explore the unknown interior of the great Island of Vancouver, then an English colony of itself, but now united with British Columbia in one government.

The country we must traverse for months to come is not inviting. Only yesterday we climbed the highest hills, and looked out on it. There it stretched, wave after wave of forest-clad hills and valley—the sea of giant pine only broken by a quiet, glassy lake, or a fiery river rushing over its rocky bed in foaming cascades, or winding in tortuous course through the silent glades, like a shining silver thread. It is in vain that we ask for some clue to that interior, so near at hand, yet, in knowledge, so far off. Trappers and hunters know nothing of it. Searching for bear or for beaver, these knight-errants of the West have gone into it a little way, trusting to luck and their good rifle, and have come back telling strange tales. Indians know less for they live on the coast, and are scared when out of sight of their villages. In awe-controlled whispers the elk-hunter tells of the strange sight he has seen, or which some equally reliable friend of his told him, about the terrible things which lurk in that great forest and by the banks of those unsearched rivers. His mythology grows rich on the fruit of such tales of wonder. Here live Indians clad in beaver-skins, by the shore of a nameless lake; Smolenko's jointless friends, who chase the hapless hunter along the mountainside; Masolemuch, who hunts by the shores of Kaatz, the great lake—pans, dryads, and hamadryads, gods of the woods, the groves, and the running streams, are all conjured up by the superstitious Indian as inhabiting that mystical, strange, untrodden interior. We have our more prosaic misgivings regarding the task we have sworn to attempt. The whole country is a dense, trackless forest, thick with underbrush and long ''drifts'' of fallen timber, through and amoung which the explorer must crawl as best he may. Every ounce of baggage—limited indeed as it is, to a minimum of *sine quâ nons*—must be carried on men's backs, and to a great extent we must depend for our subsistance on the chance product of the hunt. Indians are frightened to go far into the interior, and the rivers can only be depended on as means to penetrate to a very limited extent, being shallow, and full of rapids and cascades, to work canoes around which, even to the most skilled of Indian pilots, is far more laborious than wearily trudging along through the swampy forest, broken by mountains and ravines, with loads on our backs.

Well-intentioned friends give us an abundance of advice, plentifully distinguished by a lack of reason or experience; and Sir Arthur Kennedy, wiser and less sanguine, tells us to do our best, and get through somehow or other. To add to our griefs, news comes in that the Indians have fallen on Waddington's men up the coast, and murdered 16 of them, who were making a trail some distance off Bute Inlet. Jocular acquaintances, therefore, discount our chances of escape on no very favourable terms, and beg us to insure our lives in their favour. Hudson Bay traders stand grinning like Mephistopheles, for they like the idea of exploration little enough, as they have a presentiment that it will not help the fur trade much, and give us Machiavelian advice in regard to our treatment of the Indians, while they prophesy—honest men—to the bystanders that we shall never come back to claim our pay. The kindly mob, however, which now lines the "Hudson Bay Wharf" at Victoria, gives us the cheap tribute of applause, the flag on the Government House is dipped, and we are cheered and re-cheered by our friends, who run along the shore until our red-shirted band, on board one of Her Majesty's vessels, disappears round arbutus-covered Ogden Point.

Captain Verney soon lands us at the mouth of the Cowichan River, where we propose to break ground; and as we pitch our camp in front of the Comiaken Indian's village, a few settlers, who have found their way along with the priest and the peltry-trader thus far into the outer world, drop in to wish us luck, and to press upon us their little hospitalities and presents. Things don't seem to open well, for no sooner is the gunboat-party out of sight than an Indian, in the full-dress of a shirt-collar and a pair of socks, is good enough to threaten to shoot the writer, when disputing about the price of a canoe, for the hire of which he has been only offered about twice the value. Circumstances, connected with muscular action, cause him to hurriedly change his mind. Old Locha is the chief of this tribe, an ancient now quite blind, but a dandy of the first water, for his nose and ear pendants of Haliotis shell must measure, each of them, more than an inch square; and as to signify to him our admiration of the purity of the nacre, he informs us that they cost three blankets each. He condescends to finish our supper, and is so highly pleased with the quality of our cook, and the kindness of his friend, the "big chief" of the white men, that he offers his youngest son—a merry-faced lad of eighteen—for service on the expedition. Old Locha was once a great warrior, and he and this child, years ago, played part in a stratagem so bloody that, as a specimen of our friend, I may relate it. The Stekins, from the far north, were the scourge of Locha's tribe. They were, and are to this day, ruthless pirates and marauders, defiant in their pride of strength, who spare neither man, women, or child of any tribe who may fall in their power. One day his messengers brought to him news that a party of Stekins were on their way to attack his village. He took a strong party of his men, and posted them in the woods about a mile from his village, leaving his little son—our newly-acquired companion, Lemo—wrapped up in a blanket in a canoe drawn up on the beach, in convenient proximity to the ambush. Suspecting nothing, the Stekins sailed up Cowichan Bay until they spied what they took for an Indian girl, left in the canoe while her mother was gathering roots and berries in the woods. They immediately paddled in shore, anxious to secure this easily-acquired slave. The little boy had, however, received his directions. Waiting until they were close at hand, in apparent fright he ran into the woods. Everyone of the Stekins was anxious to catch him, and accordingly, leaving their canoes on the beach, they ran into the woods after him; but the little boy was too nimble for them. Returning to the beach they were horrified to find themselves unarmed and defenseless, surrounded by Locha and his warriors. It is said that every one of them was either killed or taken prisoner. "They absolutely cried, the dogs!" the old man tells us with contemptuous flourish of his knife, "when we commenced to cut off their heads. Ugh!"

In the morning our very modest baggage is sent up the river with some Indians in a canoe, and one of our party to see that they forgot not the distinction between meum and tuum, while we ourselves take to the bank, and soon lose sight of the settlers who come out to the door to cheer us as we pass. We are soon amid tall forests, where the only sound that breaks on the ear is the echo of our own voices, the tap! tap! of Gairdner's woodpecker (*Picus gairdneri*), or the distant sound of some pioneer woodsman's axe. A trodden forest path is seen: following this, we suddenly emerge in front of a large Indian village, comprising of long rows of squared board lodges on either side of the shelving river banks, and crowds of red-skins, old and young, come out to look at the intruders on their rightful domain.

THE INTERIOR

The Indian village on whose quietude we had thus intruded had green maples and alders shading the houses, giving it a pleasant look. Thus far Indian life in the heyday of summer and plenty-looked pleasant enough. But all around the village is "an ancient and fish like smell"—an odour of salmon in all stages of decay—for it is also the height of the salmon-fishing season. There is a weir of upright poles, with oblong boxes, made of an open-work of cedar rods, with their open mouths to the current, suspended from its base; while canoes dash hither and thither with the eager fishermen. An Indian, stark naked, stands over a pool, and now and again spears a silvery salmon, numbers of which are lying quivering on the bank beside him. In the lodges, families are sitting round the fires, boiling and eating "sabud" to their stomach's content; greasy-looking youngsters have scarcely energy enough to peer out of their fat-encompassed eyes at the "King George men" who have—rare event—come on a visit to them. I am not long here before certain old worthies suddenly recollect that they knew me once before, or that they rendered some service to somebody or other—date and circumstances not very clear—the end of which is, of course, a plug of tobacco or a pipeful of paint.

Glad to escape from the multitude of friends, we file out of Quamichan (the hump-back country), as from the contour of the surrounding hills is called, and again have only the tall pines and the whirring grouse for our company. Afternoon is far advanced when we reach the highest Indian village on the Cowichan River—called Tsamena ("the upper place")—and as we have here fixed our rendezvous, we pitch camp and make ourselves at home until our river party arrives. Tsamena is a quiet place, a sort of fishy edition of the "Deserted Village," and a few old folks loaf about with an air of departed grandeur. Amoung the shady trees behind the village we see carved figures and quaint sculpturings on the graves, and many of the graves seem new, and the figures betoken a taste acquired since civilization has got on their borders. Sometimes a man is represented with a hat on, while on other pillers, supporting a box into which the body is doubled, the owl-emblem of the departed—is rudely carved.

Old Kakalatza, the chief, is soon introduced to us: a quiet old man, who sits in front of our little tent-door talking in a subdued way, almost under his breath. "You had many people in your village?" I ask him. "Very famous were the warriors of Tsamena in old Tsosieten's wars?" "Ah, Yes!" is the reply in the careless, off-hand way of these Indians; "but some are gone to Victoria, and some are hunting on the hills, and some are gathering gamass[1], others are fishing at the salt water, while others are gone—when they go there they never come back again;" and we felt sorry for the old man, as he pointed with his thumb over his shoulder to the last resting-place of the warriors of Tsamena. Kakalatza is a great hunter, and every year goes into the interior to hunt elk, by the borders of the great lake out of which this river arises; he agrees to go with us and take his canoe along with him, to convey our stores, so that suddenly a heavy source of anxiety is removed from our minds.

Whilst we were sitting down to supper in the course of the same evening, a strange-looking recruit for our expedition turned up, and in broken Red-River French, offered his services as hunter to M'sieur le Capitaine. As he sat apart on a log, his solitary hand in his pocket, a more unpromising looking character could not well be imagined. He was no less a man than "One-armed Tomo" or Thomas, famous amoung hunters and trappers all the way from Vancouver Island to Rupert's Land, and of late years not unknown to Her Majesty's courts of justice in a rather compromising light. His father was an Iroquois voyageur from Canada, his mother a Chinook from the Columbia River. He had for forty years moved about over the country amoung

1 The bulbs of *Gamassia esculenta*, much used as an article of food by the Indians.

Hudson Bay forts and hunting stations—voyageur, farmer, hunter, trapper—possibly worse; speaking every Indian language and most European ones, so far as he had met with everybody to teach him; very often "wanted," but rarely to be found; half Indian, half white; a north-western polyglot interpreter, doing a little of everything—some things very well. Under more favourable circumstances he would have been an admirable Crichton. As it was, One-armed Tomo was only a roving vagabond, to whom an expedition of this sort was just a windfall; and though I had been particularly warned to give a wide berth to this same north-western genius, yet, at that time being very much in want of his accomplishments, I risked the engaging of him on trial for a few weeks. Amoung our motley crew Tomo was not long in finding an old acquaintance, who promised to become guarantee for him, and before evening was over he delighted us all by the versatility of his accomplishments. Story after story dropped from his ready tongue; jokes in English, jeux desprit in French, and slow sonorous proverbs in Spanish, were rattled off in quick succession; while he kept up a by-talk with the Indians, who appeared to half fear, half admire him. Tomo's outfit was not extensive. He stood 5 feet odd in his ragged trousers and woollen shirt; a grey cap was set jauntily on his head, and a pair of wooden-soled boots, made by himself, were on his feet. More than that he had not. He borrowed a blanket from his friend the chief, and we supplied him with a rifle; so he declares with a very big oath, as he squints along the barrel, that "he is a man once more," and in two minutes is asleep under a tree, with the gun between his legs. During all our long connection none of us had ever reason to regret the day when he joined our party, and to this hour One-armed Tomo, the swarthy vagabond of the western forests, is only remembered as a hearty fellow—prince of hunters and doctor of all woodcraft—whose single arm was worth more than most men's two, and without whose help the map of Vancouver would have been but a sorry blank yet, and the first Exploring Expedition a forgotten affair.

Next morning we are astir, and off before the sleepy villagers are about. Our river party is now well organized, though every hour the labour is getting more severe as the current becomes more rapid. Four men, with long poles, swing it up stream, and hard work it is. Scarcely less severe are our labours on land. Our pathway leads through a tangled forest, until all track disappears, and we steer by the river. Sometimes we trudge pleasantly over a green, fern-covered prairie, shut in by forest, and through which a purling stream runs to join the river. Here our old desire for a "lodge in some vast wilderness" revives, and we plan out in Alnaschar-like dreams, the day when we will leave the cares of the world and science behind, and settle in this little western oasis, while our surveyor—much more practical, if less poetical—jots down that "Prairie No. 1 contains so many acres, has stony soil, but is well watered and wooded, and might possibly yield crops in the better part." Rare, however, are these little open stretches, for dense pine forests seem to prevail everywhere. Often drifts of timber lie athwart our path for several hundred yards, and we either "coon it" along the tops of the fallen trees, or creep on all fours through the dense underbrush until we regain open ground. Grouse are in abundance, and partridges, as they are called here—or sometimes willow-grouse (*Bonasia sabinii*)—flew up amoung the ferns, taking to trees and bushes the moment they are flushed. If a man is hungry, and inclined to be of a pot-hunting rather than a sportsmanlike temperament, then it is easy enough with a revolver to clean a bush of them, simply by commencing at the bottom and finishing off with the birds in the topmost branches. This treeing of grouse is quite common in Canada and in some portions of the Northern States, and in these dense forests renders pointers quite useless. On the prairies it is not so bad, but in the wooded country, to the west of the Cascade Mountains, any open country is very uncommon. We are not remarkably conscientious how we get our larder filled, so long as it is filled, and accordingly before evening not a few grouse have fallen to our pistols. The sun is getting low, and as we think of making for the river, to see if our canoe is not at hand, we hear the report of a gun, and in a few minutes, emerging by the side of a little lake, bright with the yellow water-lily, we find our canoe party busy preparing supper. They are encamped on a little prairie, close by an old Indian lodge; the fire is blazing away right merrily and while Buttle is making tea, Tomo is skinning a deer, which he has shot, and the son of the war-like Locha is boiling beans, flavoured with wild onions and grouse eggs. Everybody is in excellent humour at the good commencement of our first day's trip into the wilds; and a good supper, whatever the record of such a materialistic affair may be thought of by people who never knew what it was to lie down without such, and know that your breakfast was yet on four legs in the woods, adds an acme to everybody's good nature. We compare notes for the day, write out our memoranda, and protract such sketches as we may have made, arrange next day's work, and, after smoking a last pipe, each man rolls himself in his red, blue, or green blanket, and before the chronometer goes round another 10 minutes, everyone is snoring away under his favourite tree, on a pile of fir twigs, most fragrant and grateful of woodland couches.

Such was our daily routine for many weeks; the land party meeting the river party at night, at some bend of the river; or, by pre-arranged signals, coming to their assistance, to help them to carry the canoe and cargo over drifts of trees, which jammed up the river in places. The river navigator was often very bad, and sometimes we had to dispatch assistance to bring the canoe alongside our camp, the canoe-men being thoroughly worn out; though at other times the land party would arrive after dark, even more exhausted than the river party. Sometimes we had to push through the bushes, wet and dripping with a continual down-pour of rain—the water literally pouring down our backs—over fallen trees, the bark of which, wet and slippery, slid from under our feet, and sending us tumbling, blanket and ''pack'' on back, into some ravine, where we might think ourselves happy did no further mishap befall us than a thorough sousing, a trifle in our then soaked condition. In such a case there was no use in putting on a wry face, for the laugh would be against us, and there was nothing but to ''grin and bear it.'' At other times we had to cross deep glens, through which a roaring mountain torrent was rushing, by a frail bridge composed of a single tree thrown over. The slightest nervousness would overbalance the traveller, and little hope could be entertained of his after safety, so that some of our more timid companions preferred prudently to work their way over astride of the log, after the operation called ''cooning'' it—ludicrous in name, and still more ludicrous in reality. Sometimes the river ran between high, rocky banks, over which we had to climb, looking down on the river party far beneath, like toy voyageurs, drawing a tiny canoe. Down in shady hollows we often came on streams where the remains of old bear-traps, and the skeleton salmon, with which they had once been baited, in them, telling that once on a time hunters had passed that way; but hitherto not a human being had crossed our path. With the exception of our companion, Kakalatza, it is now rarely that anybody troubles these wilds, though certain signs pointed out by the old Indian, told him that somebody had passed that way not long before, and profiting by past experiences, he would, after his own fashion, write directions or warnings for them on the smooth-barked trees, which would catch their eyes. There, with a bit of red chalk which he had picked up amoung the party, he would mark a ford, where the foot traveller could cross, by the rude sketch of a man carrying a load above his head; and at a bad rapid, it would be a canoe turned upside down; as a sort of postcript, he would add the information that we had passed by there on or about such a time of the moon, by chalking out a half-moon, nine figures with ''chimney-pot'' hats (the universal savage sign for a white man), two figures without hats, and one without an arm; and lastly, with an internal chuckle, a something by which he meant to represent a thievish, one-eyed, stump-tailed cur, which one of our party shared his meals with, and which was kicked by everybody else. None of the Indians on this coast—unless Kakalatza is an exception, and really I think the knowledge on his part was an invention of his own—know anything of the sign-writing of the Eastern American Indians, and little of any sign language, except a few contemptuous shrugs or grimaces, though at Cape Flattery I saw among the Indians there a family who knew how to communicate their thoughts by means of signs in writing, some specimens of which I possess. The study of these had induced the author, and others better able to judge such matters, to believe that these were learned from a party of Japanese seamen, who were wrecked at Cape Flattery in 1836, and lived for some time amoung the Indians; but the discussion of this point would lead us into matters foreign to the nature of this article, and must be reserved for another place. Old Kakalatza was quite a study in his way. Some time or another an English dandy, who had found his way to the confines of his village, had presented Kakalatza with a superfine black silk hat, and a hat-box, the former owner having no need for such civilized superfluities in so westerly a longitude. In course of time the old man began to regard this hat and hat-box in the light of his guarantees of respectability, and accordingly when he went with us the hat-box was put into the canoe, either out of an idea that the possession of it would impress us with awe, or that he was afraid to endanger the peace of his village by leaving such a valuable piece of property unprotected in his lodge. However, on Sunday mornings he would carefully give himself the usual weekly wash, comb out his long, raven locks (with his fingers), paint a streak of red down the bridge of his nose, and three others of a similar nature radiating from either cheek, draw his blanket about him, and finally, putting on his tall hat (which was rather of an ancient "fashion"), he would sit under a giant pine dignified enough for a sachem. Kakalatza was a pious man, as Indians go (he had not killed a man, he told

us, for six months, and as he had lately joined the Catholic
Church, I had once thought of constituting him domestic
chaplain to the expedition; but on consulting the ex-
clergyman of our party, he gravely assured me that, looking at
the matter from a business point of view, he did not consider
the man worth the 50 cents a Sunday extra which he
demanded for his services, and that, moreover, if there were
any burying to do—baptisms and marriages were out of the
question—he himself would be glad to do it for his tobacco.

Sunday was generally voted a day of rest, and I regret to
say was looked upon by the astronomer of the party as a
favourable time for getting sights for the errors of the
chronometers, and by everybody else for mending and
washing clothes, and generally bringing up leeway for the
week past. It was very pleasant on these quiet summer evenings
as we lay around the blazing fire, talking of the past and the
future—for we were all young enough to look to a future—and
all of us old enough and experienced enough of the world to
have a tale of the past to tell. There were men round that camp
fire whose lives were a romance, and it was only years
afterwards that I accidentally learned how weird a tale one at
least could have told; but here, far in the interior of the
unknown land, he lay dreamily smoking, and thinking of the
former days when his name was not unknown to fame. It was
on these occasions that old Kakalatza, through an ever-ready
interpreter, would tell his tales of war, and of love, and of the
forest glade; tales, some of which are now embalmed in
American mythology, and smoked and theorised over by
dreamy German savans, who, I fear, make more of them than
either the teller or the recorder ever did. Every dark pool
suggested a story to him, every living thing had a superstition,
and hour after hour we lay awake listening to the strange story
of Kakalatza, Lord of Tsamena.

Not a wit less backward is our one-armed hunter, whose
head is full of such lore. The men to whom all this is novel, lie

in the tent doors listening and questioning with fresh interest; while those who are already initiated in such matters are equally alert to commentate and criticise. It is the only amusement of the men, and far be it from the Commander by any act of his to discourage their mirth and good spirits, if they choose to spend their leisure hours in this manner. Men are only too apt to get what they call "down in the mouth," without their leader by any foolish wish of his to exercise a tyrannical authority over their habits, adding to or inducing it. So they lie talking and laughing, and listening and wondering, until the fire burns low, and Tomo is preparing to get sleep under his tree, his only preparation for that event—as indeed with all of us—being to take off his boots. But fresh wood is thrown on the embers, and as the gladsome blaze lights up the forest and scares the owls from their roosting places, the cry is raised, "Give us another story, Tomo;" and the sage-man of the northwest continues his tales far into the night.

ACROSS THE ISLAND

Such were our nightly amusements in these solitudes. Tomo's voice is rather cracked with northern blasts and "Hudson Bay rum," but it is loud enough, and a hoot! hoot! from the branches of a Douglas fir echoed back the notes of the wild songs he used to sing. Both the Indians speak low when the voice of an owl is heard in the solitude, for, like all men who lead lives such as theirs, they are very superstitious. According to them, the owl is the personification of dead men; when men die, their spirits, by transmigration, pass into the owl; and if the dreaded note of the bird is heard at night, it is a sign that we must have offended the dead by speaking about them. Hence, an Indian will rarely mention the name of a dead man, but only refer to him in a roundabout way. The raven is also a bird of superstition with the Indians, as it is all the world over. "The raven that croaked on Duncan's battlements." was no more a bird of ill *omen* than the black fishy fellow who sits caw-ing on the salmon drying poles round an Indian village in Vancouver Island. Soothsayers presage the weather by him, and old men will be pointed out who have foretold war and disaster to their tribesman by the croaking of the raven. Tomo pretends always to be able to foretell the rains by its croaking, though Mr. Leech of our party declares that he often catches him looking at the falling of my Aneroid barometer, which possibly in his wandering life he has learned to be more accurate in its indications of weather change than his black friend overhead.

Here are examples of other myths. The moon appears behind the clouds —"Ah! there is a frog in the moon." cries Tomo, and as the stars twinkle out one by one, we hear their names; how the Pheiades are a group of fishes; how the constellation of Ursa Major is three men in a canoe, and so on. Most of the stars are little people, and we hear the widespread Indian tale of the two girls who were spirited up into the sky by Castor and Pollux, and how they finally escaped by digging a hole in the vault of heaven and letting themselves down by a rope of cedar bark. If you doubt it, is not there the rope coiled up yet on Knockan Hill near Victoria—all in good trap rock? I am interested in this little tale, for in one form or another it is world wide, and in Europe finds its counterpart in "Jack and the Bean Stalk." A log covered with the sweet-rooted fern[2] drifts down the river at our feet. This is the old women who came "sweet-hearting" her granddaughters, two wanton girls who lived in a lodge all by themselves, and who, when they found out the gay gallant who came a-wooing to be only their old grandmother in disguise, got so enraged that they threw her into the river. A splash is heard in the water. It is only a mink very early out after a

---

2 *Popypedium vulgare*

breakfast, or very late a supper-hunting. But the mink was not always a mink. He was once a boy who went so far off in his canoe that he came to a country where people lived on Iogua shells,[3] sailed on copper canoes, and had their lodge doors also of the same metal. On his way back he met with a mishap and got swallowed up by a whale; which, however, soon tired of its bargain and vomited him up very hungry on the shore. He saw sea eggs (*echini*) at the bottom, and dived repeatedly for them, making a hearty meal. Now, he met Haelse, who asked him for some, but the boy told him that he had better dive for some himself, so Haelse threw water in his face, and told him that he would dive forever. So he became a mink. Haelse is the Hiawatha of these Indians, and is a miraculous being, to those agency all wonderful things are ascribed. He seems to be of the nature of a supreme being, and is found under some name in every Indian tribe that I know anything about. He made the beaver, who was a boatman on a lake, into its present shape, because he disobeyed him; but he also gave it power to make rains to fill its dams.

Sometimes we are startled by a wild, weird-like cry which comes out of the mist in the swamp on the other side of the river. ''Ah!'' cry both our Indians together; ''that must be Pequoichen, the one-eyed giant, and his slave, the loon, ferrying some poor hunter across to his lodge.'' Then, in explanation of their meaning, follows a wild tale of wonder. The long howl of the wolf strikes on our ear, then the gathering cry, and we retreat to our tents for arms, and heap more fuel on the fire; a rush is heard and a splash in the river, followed by a pack of hungry wolves. It is a deer hotly pursued. ''That must be,'' old Kakalat-za thinks, ''Stuckeia, the wolf man.'' He was a hunter who was converted into a wolf, and when last seen was hunting with the pack in the mountains. Then follows a long string of traditions about hunters who were converted into animals whilst ''seeking

3 *Dentalium preciosum*, the ''Indian money.''

their medicines;'' of the lightning eye potentate who once lived on the top of Salt Spring Island, and a dozen other such like legends. And so the talk goes on, until the golden sheen of the sun glimmers through the trees, dissipating the fog from the river and the wooded hills, and, after the "gruesome talk" we have been indulging in, looking like a messenger from a better world. "Etsina" Kakalatza exclaims, "there is the sun-seam seakum—a great traveller is my lord the sun—a very great traveller—much greater than you!" and here he grimly nods to a member of our party who had already grown rather famous as a teller of wonderful travellers' tales, and with the laugh which follows this sally, those of our little camp who are not already snoring lustily under the trees or in the tent, turn in to get a few hours of sleep, and dream of medicine-men and ogres, until at six the cook rouses all hands for breakfast. We wash in the river, dress at random as far as we are not already dressed, and lustily attack the beans and side of venison roasting at the fire, and then, loading the canoe, each man—commander, artist, astronomer, or pioneer, for there are no servants here (thank heaven)—shoulders his "swag" and is off through the lonely woods, rousing up the deer from their lair amoung the fern, salal, and huckleberry bushes.

The forests through which we travel are composed of gigantic firs, every tree fit for the spear of a Titan, or the "mast of some great admiral." Few of them less than 250 feet in height, and are straight as arrows, unbranched for sixty or seventy feet. We were, however, little inclined for the admiration of them, for during this part of our march the rain fell without intermission. Still we jogged on in dogged stubbornness, just like men who do not care what turns up; things cannot be much worse. We were wet enough for two days' drying, and the water ran down in little streams at the foot of our trousers' legs. We were cold outside and inside, and the camp was out of meat. Not a deer was to be seen ambling amoung the wet bushes, and I dare say our muskets were as wet as their owners. No grog was ever carried on any expedition I had ever the control of, not even, had we the means to convey it, would any wise man, knowing the material of western expeditions, ever venture into the woods with such combustible material in his possession. And how our clothes were to be dried puzzled us. We had tents though we rarely erected them. The erection, however, was quick enough. While some of the men are unloading the canoe, four others spring into the brush with the hatchets, and almost quicker than I have written the words, five thin poles are cut, our ridge-pole tent erected, and the fire is blazing before the camp kettle is filled with water for our refreshing tea. However, the wood is all soaked to-night—this fatal 12th of June, even if the fire would light amid such a pour. Suddenly we hear the rushing sound of a waterfall, and crashing through amoung nettles (sure signs of human abodes), to our delight and astonishment we land in front of a pretty waterfall, with remains of salmon pots and old lodges choked up with nettles on the other side of the river. Two others in good repair are on this side, and though a canoe is at the landing, the lodges do not seem to have been tenanted for long. They are, however, warm and pleasant, though smelling strongly Indian, and we hail them as a lucky find. Soon, with great delight, we take possession of the best, and have a fire blazing in the middle in readiness for the arrival of our canoe. Kakalatza soon comes in with the air of a man at home, grins us a welcome, and tells us that this is one of his regular hunting lodges. The canoe no doubt belongs to some Masolemucha, a tribe of Indians who occasionally hunt on the great lake, and once possessed the ruined lodge on the other side of the river. We afterwards found that these Indians (of whom we heard wonderful tales on the coast) are a section of the Nittenahts, a western tribe, and that this canoe belonged to their chief, who preferred to pass this way to the east coast, rather than risk the stormy shores of the De Fucas Strait in the spring season. He is off trading somewhere, and is not yet back. Kakalatza, who does not care much for our tea and boiled beans, climbs up into the rafters of the lodge, and brings forth a quantity of dried elk's meat, which he had deposited here against some such chance. We soon strip off our inexpressibles, and hang them up to dry with our wet shirts. Our pack supplies a spare shirt, and the blanket, Indian fashion, completes our garments. In this half-savage guise our artist sketches us, and as the picture was, I regret to say for colonial taste, much more popular than views of fine scenery, it now ornaments not a few far western parlours, where, possibly at the moment I am writing, some good friends of ours are laughing at what they were pleased to call "Brown's savages." Now it is that Kakalatza, his heart warmed with fire and elk's meat, sweet tea and boiled beans, relaxes into familiarity, and his wrinkled old face beams with something like a self-satisfied smile, as he glances round the lodge and recalls a little reminiscence connected with it. We are all at our ease, reclining in our blankets, around the roaring fire, and listen to him.

One night, just such a night as this, some years ago, he was hunting up this river, and on entering this lodge he was surprised to find a woman crouching in the corner. She was a Nuchultaw, from Suckwhanotan, the Rapid's village, in Discovery Passage, and had been a slave with the Callams, on the other side of De Fucas Strait, for a number of years. Yearning for home, she and another woman of the same tribe determined to attempt their escape. They only knew that the direction of their home was somewhere on the other side of the range of mountains they saw on the Vancouver shore, and that beyond lay a river (the Cowichan) by which they might reach the coast, and so northward. Accordingly, one dark night they stole a canoe, and alone crossed the strait, took to the woods and travelled by the sun. Probably no human beings had ever penetrated these mountains before, and how laborious the journey must have been may be gathered from the fact that a well-equipped party of experienced travellers, sent by me to explore the same route, took more than a week to traverse it. While descending a a precipice, one of the women fell and fractured her leg. Her companion could do nothing for her, so leaving her to the certain fate which awaited her, she pursued her perilous and laborious journey, finally arriving at the river and travelling down it. She had sought shelter in the hut, where our friend Kakalatza had found her.

The old fellow stopped in his narrative. ''What did you do with her?'' we all eagerly inquired, impressed with the heroism of the woman. A curious sinister smile played around the leathern features of the chivalrous savage, as he replied, ''Went home again, and sold her to the Lummi Indians for eighty blankets!''

On the 15th of June the river began to get calm and lakelike, and to our great delight, turning a bend, we came in sight of a large and beautiful lake, stretching away amoung wooded hills in solitary grandeur. This was the source of the river and here for a pleasant week or more we fixed our headquarters, rambling all around the neighboring country. Summer was now come in all its Italian beauty; the skies were sunny and clear, and all Nature was blooming as brightly as she only can do in a north-western summer.

The forests were fragrant with the piny odour; the large white flowers of the dogwood (*Cornus nuttallii*) were reflected in the little glassy bays of the lake; woodpeckers tapped the trees merrily; grouse drummed in the woods; hummingbirds (*Selasphourus rufus*) darted like winged gems of emeralds and rubies amoung the flowering currant bushes; while the lordly-looking bald-headed eagle (*Haliaetus leucocephalus*) sat perched on the topmost branch of some giant fir, now and then swooping down to draw a trout from the lake. These were halcyon days. The woods echoed with our loud joyous laugh and song, and the hills with the report of the hunters' rifles; there was nothing to make us uneasy. One party surveyed the lake, which was twenty-two miles long, and from a mile to a mile and a half broad; while another under my own charge explored the wooded mountains of the Kennedy range, overlooking the lake, in search of minerals and mines. It was not often that we were separated for many days, and at night the woods and the glassy surface of the little lake bays were lit up with our camp fires; so large, indeed, that they generally defeated their purpose. "Just like the white men," old Kakalatza would growl, "they build a fire to warm themselves, and then make it so big that they can't get round it! Etsina!" Our savage was, however, in his element. He was long after heard to declare that he called "the xplorin' xpedition was the finest thing he had ever been on: good pay, not over heavy work, and plenty to eat—plenty, plenty!" The hills around the great lake were the home of our friend for six weeks or more every year. In the autumn he came up with his family and squaw to hunt elk. Elk were so abundant that on one occasion he chased seven into a rocky gulch, out of which they could not escape, so he and his sons just shot them down. He then erects frames to smoke their meat. We often saw them in the mountains during our wanderings; and after he has accumulated what he considers enough for the winter use, he makes baskets to contain it and commences to transport it to his canoe on the lake. This he does slowly and by frequent journeys, until at last he sails out of the lake, and runs the rapid river; and after many laborious portages, arrives in glee at the Tsamena village.

At last, on the 23rd of June, to fulfill the plan of exploration which I had marked out, we separated, Lieutenant Leech going with one-half of the men to the country south of the lake, with orders to meet us at Port San Juan, on De Fuca Strait; while, with the rest, I proceeded to the end of the lake, before dispatching our faithful Indian henchmen to their homes. On our way we met two canoes almost loaded with berries, containing three hunters of Tsamena on their way to the Cowichan River. Here we paid off our friends, Lemo and Kakalatza, as the one had to go back with his canoe, and the former to get married to a swarthy brunette of Quamichan village, regarding whom I had long been the repository of many secret, sighing tales. Their joy and gratitude knew no bounds, and while Kakalatza only grinned with satisfaction as he contemplated the little presents we gave them on parting, Lemo burst out with many promises. He told me that when he saw me in Victoria (he would know me by my beard, he said) he would give me some grouse, as I was his very good friend; and turning to one of our party, whom he supposed to have cast sly glances at some black-eyed half-blood of his acquaintance, he spoke with a vehemence that put the lover to the blush: "Nika wa-wa Maly copa mika;" and turning to another, "Spose Maly halu tikke yaka, mika wa-wa yaka hyou copa mika." ("I will speak to Mary for you," and "Suppose Mary will not have him, I will speak plenty to her about you.") We thanked them both for their promised good offices—epicurean and matrimonial and after watching them sailing over the lake, whence came echoing back, as far as we could see them, the shouts of farewell, we fire a parting salute, and take to the woods with a view to reach the opposite coast.

THE RETURN TO VICTORIA

After two day's easy travel through the usual wooded country, we reached a swift, narrow river flowing to the southward. This we concluded to be the Nittinat River, which, according to chart, must debouch into a lake. We now set to work to build a raft out of the dry cedar trees on the shore, with a view to descend it, as the banks were high in some places, and densely wooded with huge pines, and underbrush. In one place I measured a Menzies spruce (*Abies menziesii*) 28 feet in circumference, and high in proportion; and a cedar 45 feet in circumference or 15 feet in diameter—just half of the diameter of the huge Wellingtonias (*Sequoia*) in California. Though the river was swift, yet it was shallow, and at the lowest state of water now; so that, after we had secured our packs on it, and launched it, frequently it stuck fast on the gravel bar of the river, and then all hands sprang into the water up to the middle, and pushed it off. Gaily and with loud shouts we descended the river, until we found that the raft was proceeding rather too swiftly, and almost before we could spring ashore, we heard the roar as of a cataract. In another minute the raft would have been sucked into a canyon of the river, and undoubtedly every one of us must have been drowned or dashed to pieces. We were, however, in time, and drew our raft into a quiet haven, where, I suppose, it is still lying. We now took to the banks, and were apparently again approaching human habitations, for a trail led along the banks of the river until it ended at a little Indian lodge, uninhabited, amoung bushes by the river side. Here we found an old canoe, which we patched with old flour sacks and pine resin until it was floatable. Next morning Mr. Barnston and I set off in this frail craft down the river, to settle matters with any Indians whom we might meet, and try to arrange about the others following, leaving them in the mean time to build a raft and make the best of their way down the rapid stream, which was now deeper than before, and broader also. The morning was dull, but off we started with a cheer, sweeping down the river at a fine rate, Barnston steering, while I knelt in the bows and staved her off rocks and logs, which threatened every moment to destroy our frail craft. The river was a continuous succession of ripples and rapids, with remains of salmon weirs, and calm, deep, lake-like reaches, through which we had to propel it with paddles. It was remarkably clear of trees, there not being more than one or two stoppages from that cause. On one occasion we ran over a rapid, in the middle of which was a tree, forming a bridge, with the lower branches dipping in the water, between two of which we ran with great rapidity. We managed, however, to do so without touching, but it was a very close shave; to use the language of our steersman, it was ''spitting through a keyhole without touching the wards.'' The river was very winding, and at every bend it seemed to be going to end; but as we swept round some wooded point, again we were disappointed. We passed many Indian lodges on either bank, but chiefly on the right; but all now deserted, though in the autumn, when the river is alive with swarms of salmon, they will be inhabited by Nittinat salmon fishers from the coast. In all, we passed eleven lodges, all separately situated, inhabited by many families, each of them surrounded by more or less open land, or shaded with mossy maples (*Acer macrophyllum*), and embossed with salmon-berry bushes[4] laden with their pleasant fruit, the entrances, however, being everywhere chocked with thickets of nettles. They were backed by magnificent forests of Hemlock[5], spruce, and cedar, though as a rule the timber decreased in quality as we approached the coast, and the forests became denser, with an undergrowth of salal (*Gaultheria shallon*) and other creeping shrubs. Several well-defined hills, though all wooded to the summit, lent variety to the scene. All day long we paddled, with only one halt, and the sun began to set, and there seemed no end of the river, though I calculated that we had followed its windings for more than twenty geographical miles.

The canoe leaked abominably, I was nearly up to my middle in water, and we had every now and then to get out to ease it over some shallow. If the chartography of the river is not very perfect, anyone who has ever sketched in such circumstances will readily forgive what he can appreciate. We were about giving up all hopes of seeing the end that day when to our delight the current decreased and a strong sea breeze began to blow; the downward current was stemmed by a slight upward one, and soon we sighted a lake-like sea, with large trees which the spring and winter freshets had brought down. We here drew our canoe ashore and lit a fire; and as night closed in we got anxious for the safety of our companions. Just as we were rolling ourselves up in our blankets, we were aroused by shouting on the river, and starting up in fear of Indians, we could scarcely credit our eyes

4 *Rubus spectabilis*. Dougl.
5 *Abies mertensiana*. Lindl.

when Whymper[6] and MacDonald landed from a raft, all safe, but drenched to the skin. They had built a raft and this being too small for the whole party, Buttle and Lewis had started down the river bank, and hoped that we would send succor to them, as they had no food whatever. It was hard to get to sleep, for MacDonald (who was an old sailor) "yarned" until morning about the wonderful decent of the river they had—on two boards out of the Indian lodge, tied together with their blanket ropes, the holes being made by firing pistol bullets through. Indeed, so wonderful was the adventure, that we have hesitated to relate it before, in case the discovery of the source of the Nile and the descent of the Nittinat, all in one year, might upset the geographical world! We were up by early dawn, and Barnston and I started off in our little canoe to seek Indians to go after Buttle and Lewis and take us all to the Nittinat village. Rounding the first point, we came right in front of an Indian village of four or five large lodges. As our canoe was leaking badly, we drew in to see if we could get another. The whole place was deserted; but in the chief's house, known by a ring of red on the outer wall, we found a tolerably good canoe, which, after the free and easy style of the north-west, and in the name of Her Majesty the Queen and her faithful deputy Arthur Edward Kennedy, we pressed into the service of the Expedition. It was rather a high-handed act, but necessity compelled it, and, moreover, the law of the stronger dictated it. We were not long in finding Lewis and Buttle, sitting rather dolefully on a "sandbar," making a meager breakfast of salmon berries. They said they had "had a hard time of it," and their torn clothing and woebegone appearance did not belie their words. We were only sorry that our larder—now sans meat, sans bread, sans tea, sans everything— could scarcely supply them with anything better, but, like Mr. Squeers' boys, we adjourned to the woods after breakfast to supplement our meagre fare with a little vegetable diet in the shape of berries. Next day we spent in patching up our canoes to face the

6 Mr. Frederick Whymper, now in San Francisco, known as the author of *Travels in Alaska* and as a contributor to *Illustrated Travels*.

sea, for we now perceived that the inlet we were on was no lake, but an arm of the sea;[7] and on the 29th of the month we were up by three a.m., and started off before the wind—as it generally blows seaward before the sun gets fully risen, and the opposite direction afterwards. We passed a village on the right, and a little further on another, built on each side of a stream, with a stockade in front. All were, however, deserted. We erected a blanket for a sail on each canoe, and we went gaily along, the artist's gorgeous railway rug, which was officiating for a sail on the first canoe, giving quite a grand appearance to our tiny fleet. At the mouth of the river the salt taste of the inlet was not perceptible, from the large quantity of fresh water which was pouring in, but now sea-weeds began to appear, and the inlet to narrow. The water was also thick with Medusce, and the rocks clustered with mussels. Indian villages, tastefully situated, were common, but hitherto we had seen no inhabitants. However, towards evening, we drew into the side, prepared our arms in case of attack—for the Nittinats bear a most infamous reputation—and after a short paddle we came to a narrow entrance, eighteen miles from the Nittinat river mouth where the sea ran through with great force. Outside we could hear the glad sound of the Pacific, and all our faces brightened at the knowledge that we had crossed the colony through a narrow and hard line of travel.

"Eh! Captain," Lewis asks me. "Πoλνφoσβoιo Θαλασσηs?" Lewis is the scholar of our party, and we indulge him any such cheap display of pedantry. We see a man cutting firewood, who at the sight of us darts off to a village we see smoking on the cliff. With strong paddling we drew into a cove out of sight of the village; but we had scarcely drawn up on the beach than we were

---

7 In my map of Vancouver Island (Petermann's Geographische Mittheilungen, 1869), anxious to keep up the Admiralty nomenclature, I have called this inlet Nittinat Lake. The name seems to have misled the engraver, for he has represented it as fresh, though the text expressly describes it as salt water.

sighted, and in five minutes surrounded by a crowd of painted savages, their faces often besmeared with blood, others blackened, but not, I was glad to see, with the war black, and nearly all with pieces of haliotis shells in their ears and the septum of the nose; all professing great joy at the arrival of white men at their village. Moquilla, the chief, was, as I expected, away from home; but his deputy was excessive in his friendship and offers of assistance. I, of course, professed to believe them all, and though he assured me that his people were of the most virtuous and honest description imaginable, I ordered all our stuff to be got under cover as soon as possible, and a sharp look-out to be kept on them; but notwithstanding all our vigilance, we discovered a few hours afterwards that they had managed to steal several articles of value. Their blankets (the sole dress of most of them) give every facility for making off with small unconsidered trifles. The women mostly wore a blanket of cedar bark, nicely woven, and a girdle of the same material, and pendant stripes, in the form of an apron. The Indian would not hear of his good friend King George's[8] great chief encamping outside his village; and though I knew what his object was, as I had some favours to get from him before I left, I had to comply with as good grace as may be, and pitch our tents in the village square. The village was perched up on the rocks around, and soon we were surrounded by a crowd of men, women and children, squatting in front of our fire, begging, pilfering and trading.

The Nittinats were once a powerful tribe, but the same decadance as amoung other tribes is everywhere perceptible, and they do not now number over 400 fighting men. However, their village is almost impregnable on the beach, and the sea entering the inlet through a narrow strait, only passable at certain stages of the tide. They are great canoe builders, and their little craft in all stages of finish were lying about the village. It was the midst of

8 The general Western Indian name for an Englishman.

the halibut season, and numbers of these fish, sliced or drying, were lying about on frames. The whole place smelt fishy and disagreeable, and we were glad when night closed in and we got clear of some of our unwelcome visitors. For the first time I considered it necessary to post sentinels, as I apprehended mischief. The lights burnt in the village all night, and stones were thrown down above our watchmen. It afterwards came out that they had intended attacking us in the dark, but were afraid of our rifles and revolvers. In the morning they were of course all sweet and pleasant; but it was with difficulty that I could obtain a canoe, and then only at a very stiff price. Every objection was thrown in our way. They could not leave; there were no Indians where we were going; and the trader in whose charge our stores were expected to be was away; but, finding that we overruled all these obstacles, we finally got off, after "potlatching" (or making presents to) half the village, and buying dried halibut against famine to a good extent. I never was so glad to get quit of an Indian village, and felt exultation as we rode through the breakers, and raising the mat sail, scudded along the coast, past Kloos (Klahus "the other" [house]), Quamadoa, Echwatess, Karleit, and Wawahadis, all villages of these people, standing in little bays on sandy beaches.

By evening we enter Port San Juan—an inlet of the sea off De Fucas Strait, along which we are sailing. On the opposite side is Washington Territory, United States, and the snow-capped Olympian range can be seen in the distance, with Mount Baker's white head towering to the eastward. In Port San Juan we see no sign of vessel with stores for us, nor of our companions, whom we had expected to meet us here. Rounding a point, we come into a little cove, when our fears of starvation are at least staved off by the sight of Indians, and out of a little block-house comes a short, merry-faced fellow, who hails us as we enter with all sorts of witticisms. This is the Indian trader, who for many long years has lived all along here, though earlier in life he was a lieutenant in the Royal Navy, under Sir John Franklin. The story of this waif of civilization is a long one, and as we sit around his fire we hear bits of it, mingled with many a wild story of the life he has led here. We pitch our tent in front of his door, and accept his apologies for his want of hospitality. A few days afterwards a ragged figure comes down the San Juan river—a mountain stream which flows in here—which we recognize to be one of our companions of a week ago. He is very hungry and very tired, and has a long tale to tell of the rough mountains they have travelled over from the Cowichan Lake to the sea. A few days afterwards the Indians find the rest, and once more we are together in the rendezvous at Port San Juan. To tell their story would be to occupy too much space. Neither can I follow our subsequent career; how we discovered the gold placers of Leech; how we crossed the country by many routes and with many fortunes—good, bad, and very indifferent; and, finally, how, as the snows were covering the hills, we landed once more in Victoria, there to receive the "thanks of Parliament," and the congratulations of our friends. The object of this article has not been to describe geographical data—these I have published elsewhere—but to attempt a little sketch, so far as our space would permit, of one of the pleasantest of our many journeying and explorations—sometimes alone, at other times, as in this case, with companions—all over the wide region west of the Rocky Mountains. Pleasant as are the recollections of this journey, a more agreeable feeling still remains to him who conducted it; and that is, that during many trials, the early friendship which united us all has never been dissolved; and that, scattered as are the companions of these days through many lands, there is none who does not look back with pleasure on his early co-partnership in North-Western travel.

COLOPHON

This second printing of A JOURNEY OF EXPLORATION ACROSS VANCOUVER ISLAND by Robert Brown was printed in the workshop of Glen Adams, which is located in the sleepy country village of Fairfield, southern Spokane County in Washington state, and one township removed from the Idaho line. The booklet was edited by Innes L. Cooper of Victoria, British Columbia. Typesetting is fourteen on sixteen Garamond, a French type face that has stood the test of time. The initial "A" used on page seven was designed by Hans Weiditz and cut by Jost de Negker in 1521. It appeared first (?) in an old book by Carl Hrachowina entitled Initialen, Alphabete und Randleisten, Verschiedener Kunstepochen, printed long ago in Germany. This Ye Galleon printing of the Robert Brown booklet was set in type by Dale LaTendresse using a model 7300 Editwriter computer photosetter. The paper stock is eighty pound Wheat. Photography/darkroom work was by Vern Stevens. The film was stripped by Pat Nigh, who also made the printing plates. The sheets were printed by Vern Stevens using a 28 inch Heidelberg press model KORS. The sheets were folded by Garry Adams using a 26x40 Baum Dial-O-Matic folding machine. Assembly and binding was by the Ye Galleon crew. This was a fun project. We had no special difficulty with the work.

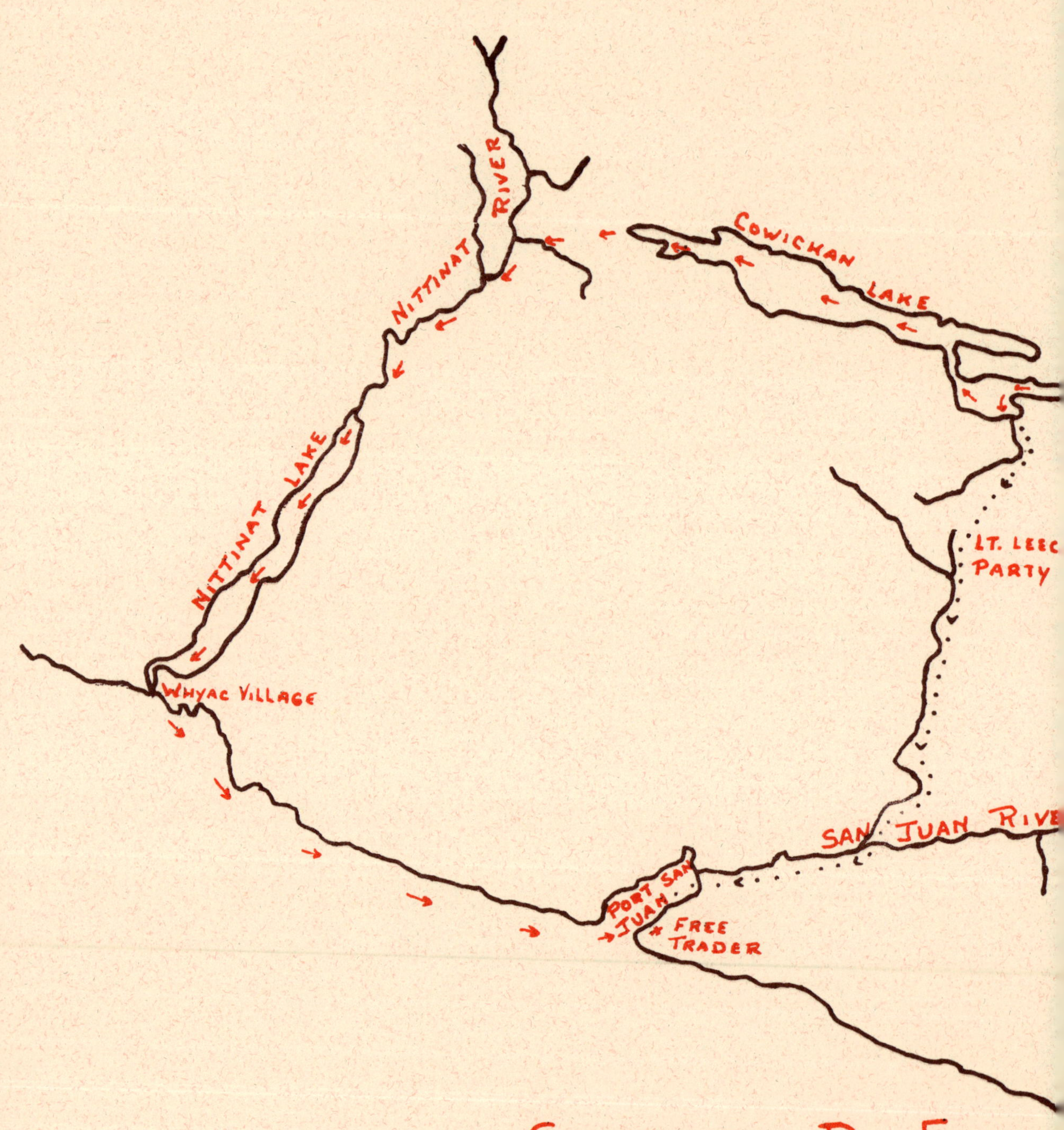

NITTINAT RIVER
NITTINAT LAKE
COWICHAN LAKE
LT. LEEC PARTY
WHYAC VILLAGE
SAN JUAN RIVER
PORT SAN JUAN
FREE TRADER
STRAITS OF DE FUCA

SALT
SPRING
ISL.
COWICHAN RIVER
VANCOUVER ISLAND
VICTORIA